The Tragic Story of Robert Brooks

Uncovering the Culture of Brutality and Racial Bias in U.S. Correctional Facilities

John M. Poulsen

Table of Contents

Introduction

A Fatal Beating Behind Bars

On December 10, 2024, Robert Brooks, a 43-year-old inmate serving time at Marcy Correctional Facility in upstate New York, was pronounced dead at Wynn Hospital in Utica. His death, initially reported as a result of "use of force" by staff, soon became a flashpoint for national outrage. Disturbing footage released by the New York Attorney General's office revealed the brutal reality: Brooks, handcuffed and defenseless, was repeatedly punched, kicked, and choked by correctional officers in what amounted to a fatal beating.

The videos, recorded by body cameras worn by some of the officers, show a sequence of shocking events. Brooks, his hands cuffed behind his back, is carried into a medical exam room by three officers. Over the next several minutes, he is assaulted—punched in the face, kicked in the groin, struck with a shoe, and ultimately left motionless on an examination table. Medical personnel stood nearby, their apparent inaction a chilling reminder of the complicity that often accompanies such violence.

As the footage circulated, it became impossible to ignore the broader systemic issues this incident laid bare. Brooks' death wasn't just a case of individual cruelty—it was emblematic of a culture of unchecked violence, racial bias, and institutional failure that permeates many American correctional facilities.

A Microcosm of a Larger Crisis

The beating and subsequent death of Robert Brooks exposed the stark realities of life behind bars in the

United States. Prisons, intended as places of rehabilitation and safety, often become sites of unchecked brutality. For decades, watchdog groups and investigative journalists have documented patterns of abuse within correctional institutions: racial disparities in treatment, the normalization of violence, and the near-impossibility of holding perpetrators accountable.

In Brooks' case, the systemic failures were clear. Four of the officers involved failed to activate their body cameras properly, rendering the footage incomplete and without audio—a common tactic to obscure wrongdoing. Despite the presence of multiple officers and medical personnel, not one person intervened to stop the attack. Instead, some appeared to watch passively, their behavior a reflection of a system that often prioritizes loyalty to staff over justice for inmates.

The Marcy Correctional Facility, where the attack took place, is no stranger to controversy. A 2022 report by the Correctional Association of New York documented widespread allegations of abuse and racial bias among its staff. The report revealed that over 70% of inmates interviewed believed that racial discrimination played a significant role in their treatment. Brooks, a Black man, became the latest victim of a system where power imbalances and prejudice often lead to deadly outcomes.

A Catalyst for Change?

Swift action from state officials have been prompted. New York Governor Kathy Hochul announced the firing of 14 correctional employees involved in the incident, including officers and a nurse. The New York Attorney General's office has opened a criminal investigation, and several advocacy groups have called for sweeping reforms to address the culture of violence in correctional facilities.

But will this be enough? The case of Robert Brooks is not an isolated incident. It is one in a long history of abuse that has gone unaddressed for far too long. His story, though tragic, presents an opportunity—a chance to confront the systemic failures that allow such brutality to persist and to demand accountability for the lives lost behind prison walls.

As this book unfolds, we will explore the Robert Brooks case in detail, shedding light on the cultural, racial, and institutional dynamics that perpetuate abuse in the correctional system. By understanding this incident within its broader context, we aim to not only honor Brooks' memory but also to spark conversations about meaningful reform.

This is not just a story about one man's death. It is a story about a system in desperate need of change.

Chapter 1

The Culture of Violence in Correctional Facilities

The heartbreaking case of Robert Brooks at Marcy Correctional Facility was not an isolated event. It was a grim reminder of the entrenched culture of violence within the U.S. correctional system—a culture where brutality is normalized, accountability is scarce, and the humanity of those incarcerated is often disregarded. Understanding how such a system came to exist requires examining its history, the role of racial bias, and the lived experiences of those who have endured its abuses.

Historical Context: How Violence Became Normalized in Prisons

Prison violence in the United States has deep historical roots. In the early days of the American penal system, incarceration was not just about serving time—it was about punishment and control. From the chain gangs of the post-Civil War South to the harsh labor camps of the early 20th century, brutality was institutionalized as part of the correctional process. Physical abuse, hard labor, and psychological torment were seen as legitimate methods of maintaining order and instilling discipline.

The 20th century saw the emergence of large, centralized prison systems, but the culture of violence persisted. Inmates who resisted authority were often subjected to beatings, solitary confinement, or worse. High-profile incidents, such as the Attica prison uprising in 1971, brought attention to the appalling conditions in many facilities. Yet, despite calls for reform, the underlying dynamics of power and control remained unchanged.

In modern times, violence in prisons is often justified under the guise of maintaining safety and order. Correctional officers are trained to use force as a last resort, but in practice, excessive force has become a first response in many institutions. Overcrowded facilities, undertrained staff, and a lack of oversight create an environment where abuse is not only tolerated but sometimes encouraged.

The Role of Racial Bias and Power Dynamics in Perpetuating Abuse

Racial bias is a pervasive and undeniable factor in the culture of violence within correctional facilities. Black and Latino inmates are disproportionately represented in the U.S. prison system, making up nearly 60% of the incarcerated population despite being less than a third of the general population. This disparity extends to how inmates are treated once they enter the system.

Studies have consistently shown that Black and Latino inmates are more likely to be subjected to disciplinary actions, solitary confinement, and physical abuse compared to their white counterparts. A 2022 watchdog report on Marcy Correctional Facility revealed that over 70% of inmates interviewed believed racial bias influenced their treatment by staff. One inmate recounted being told by an officer, "You don't get to have rights in here."

The racial dynamics within prison staff further exacerbate these disparities. Many correctional facilities, particularly in rural areas, employ predominantly white staff members to oversee a largely nonwhite inmate population. This racial divide often fuels mistrust and creates an "us versus them" mentality, where inmates are dehumanized and seen as threats to be controlled rather than individuals to be rehabilitated.

Power dynamics within prisons also play a significant role in perpetuating abuse. Correctional officers wield immense authority over inmates, with the ability to dictate nearly every aspect of their daily lives. This power imbalance, combined with a lack of effective oversight, creates an environment where abuses can occur with little fear of reprisal. Officers who engage in misconduct are often protected by their unions, and internal investigations rarely result in meaningful consequences.

Testimonies from Former Inmates and Whistleblower Officers

The voices of those who have lived and worked within the prison system offer a stark glimpse into its violent underbelly. Former inmates describe a world where fear and brutality are part of daily life.

Darnell, a former inmate who served time at a medium-security prison in upstate New York, recounted an incident where an officer slammed another inmate's head against a wall for not moving quickly enough during a count. "He wasn't resisting or anything," Darnell said. "But the officer just kept yelling, 'You don't get to decide when we're done.'" The inmate was left bleeding and dazed, but no report was filed, and the officer faced no consequences.

Maria, another former inmate, described a similar environment of unchecked aggression. "If you complained about anything, they'd throw you in the hole," she said, referring to solitary confinement. "Sometimes they didn't even tell you why. It was just to show you who was in charge."

Even correctional officers have spoken out about the culture of violence, though many do so anonymously for fear of retaliation. One whistleblower officer from a southern state described how new recruits were often pressured to conform to the "code" of silence. "If you don't back up your fellow officers, you're the one who gets ostracized," he said. "And if someone's stepping out of line, you're expected to stay quiet or join in."

This code of silence not only protects abusive officers but also isolates those who want to challenge the status quo. Many officers who attempt to report misconduct find themselves targeted for harassment or reassigned to undesirable posts.

A System in Need of Change

The culture of violence in correctional facilities is not an accident—it is the result of decades of systemic failures, racial inequalities, and unchecked power. Incidents like the fatal beating of Robert Brooks are not anomalies; they are the predictable outcome of a system that prioritizes control over rehabilitation, punishment over justice.

To dismantle this culture, systemic change is necessary. This includes increasing transparency, holding abusive staff accountable, and fostering an environment where rehabilitation and respect are at the forefront of correctional practices. The voices of former inmates and whistleblower officers must be amplified, and their experiences used as a guide to create a prison system that values humanity over brutality.

The road to reform is long, but as the following chapters will show, it is a journey we must undertake if we are to ensure that what happened to Robert Brooks never happens again.

Chapter 2

The Failure of Oversight and Accountability

The footage of Robert Brooks' fatal beating at Marcy Correctional Facility was shocking not only for the brutality it exposed but also for what it lacked. The absence of audio in the body camera recordings underscored a glaring issue: the failure of oversight and accountability within the U.S. correctional system. While body-worn cameras have become a symbol of transparency, their misuse—or outright manipulation—reveals the deep flaws in ensuring justice for inmates. Beyond cameras, a system riddled with weak investigations, protective unions, and institutional inertia makes holding correctional staff accountable a near-impossible task.

Body Camera Usage: A Tool Undermined by Misuse

Body-worn cameras were introduced in many correctional facilities as a measure to increase transparency and accountability. Their purpose is clear: to document interactions between inmates and staff, deter abuse, and provide evidence for investigations. In theory, these cameras are a game-changer. In practice, however, their impact is often undermined by misuse and systemic loopholes.

Deactivation and Audio Failures

In the case of Robert Brooks, four of the officers involved were wearing body cameras. Yet none of the footage captured audio of the assault. Why? Because the officers failed to activate their cameras properly, a common occurrence in such incidents. While the video alone revealed shocking levels of brutality, the absence of sound left significant gaps in understanding the context—what was said, what orders were given, and how events escalated.

This is not an isolated issue. Across the country, officers have been found deactivating cameras during critical moments or failing to turn them on altogether. Some agencies allow officers to activate cameras manually, creating opportunities for selective recording. Even when automatic activation policies exist, officers have found ways to circumvent them, such as by removing batteries or obscuring the lens.

Lack of Consequences for Misuse

Despite policies mandating body camera usage, enforcement is often lax. Officers who fail to activate cameras or tamper with recordings rarely face significant consequences. The lack of accountability for these failures erodes public trust and undermines the very purpose of the technology.

Technological and Policy Gaps

Body cameras also face technical limitations. For instance, they often have limited storage capacity, forcing agencies to delete footage after a set period—sometimes before investigations can even begin. Moreover, the lack of standardized policies across states and facilities means that how and when cameras are used varies widely, creating inconsistencies in accountability.

The Challenges of Investigating and Prosecuting Misconduct

Even when evidence of misconduct exists, holding correctional staff accountable remains an uphill battle. Internal investigations are plagued by conflicts of interest, and external oversight is often hamstrung by bureaucratic hurdles and political resistance.

Internal Investigations: A Flawed Process

In most correctional facilities, allegations of staff misconduct are handled internally by departments like the Office of Special Investigations (OSI). While these departments are tasked with ensuring impartiality, their close ties to the institutions they oversee often create a conflict of interest. Investigators may hesitate to take action against colleagues, fearing backlash or professional consequences.

This reluctance is exacerbated by the "blue wall of silence"—an unwritten code among officers to protect one another at all costs. Whistleblowers who attempt to report misconduct often face retaliation, from harassment to reassignment to undesirable posts. This culture of silence makes it nearly impossible for investigations to proceed fairly.

Union Protections and Arbitration

Correctional officers' unions wield significant power, often shielding members from accountability. Disciplinary actions against officers frequently result in arbitration, where independent mediators can overturn decisions. This process, while intended to protect workers' rights, often undermines efforts to hold abusive staff accountable.

For example, in New York, correctional officers have been reinstated after being fired for egregious misconduct, including violence against inmates. The arbitration process frequently prioritizes procedural errors over the substance of the allegations, allowing guilty officers to return to work.

Prosecutorial Challenges

Prosecuting correctional officers for misconduct is even more difficult. District attorneys, who often work closely with law enforcement agencies, may be reluctant to pursue cases against officers. Additionally, juries tend to sympathize with officers, viewing their actions as necessary to maintain order in a dangerous environment.

Without strong evidence—such as clear video and audio recordings—it becomes nearly impossible to secure convictions. This creates a vicious cycle: officers act with impunity, knowing that the system is unlikely to hold them accountable.

Insights from Watchdog Reports and Investigative Journalism

Journalistic investigations and watchdog organizations have played a crucial role in exposing the failures of oversight in correctional facilities. Their findings paint a damning picture of a system designed to protect itself rather than the people it incarcerates.

Revelations from Watchdog Reports

The Correctional Association of New York, an independent watchdog group, has documented widespread abuse and neglect in state prisons. Their 2022 report on Marcy Correctional Facility revealed troubling patterns of violence, racial bias, and staff misconduct. Four out of five inmates interviewed reported witnessing or experiencing abuse by staff, with many describing physical violence as a routine occurrence.

These reports also highlight systemic failures in oversight. At Marcy, for instance, audits of body camera usage were infrequent, and staff members were rarely disciplined for misconduct. Such findings underscore the need for stronger external oversight and stricter enforcement of accountability measures.

The Role of Investigative Journalism

Investigative journalists have been instrumental in bringing abuses to light, often uncovering stories that would otherwise remain hidden. A 2015 New

York Times investigation revealed that Black and Latino inmates in New York prisons were disciplined at twice the rate of their white counterparts, often for minor infractions. More recently, The Marshall Project has chronicled the pervasive culture of violence and impunity in correctional facilities nationwide.

These investigations not only expose individual acts of misconduct but also highlight the systemic issues that allow such behavior to persist. By amplifying the voices of inmates, whistleblowers, and advocates, they shine a spotlight on the urgent need for reform.

A Broken System in Need of Repair

The failures of oversight and accountability in the U.S. correctional system are deeply entrenched. Body cameras, while a step in the right direction, are only as effective as the policies and enforcement mechanisms that accompany them. Investigations and prosecutions remain hampered by conflicts of interest, union protections, and systemic inertia.

Addressing these issues will require bold action, including:

- **Mandating Automatic Body Camera Activation:** Ensuring that cameras are always recording during interactions with inmates.
- **Strengthening External Oversight:** Establishing independent bodies to investigate allegations of misconduct.
- **Reforming Union Protections:** Balancing workers' rights with the need for accountability.
- **Increasing Transparency:** Releasing footage and reports to the public in a timely manner.

The death of Robert Brooks serves as a grim reminder of the consequences of inaction. Without meaningful reform, the cycle of violence and impunity will continue, leaving countless others to suffer in silence. The next chapter will delve into how racial disparities further exacerbate these systemic issues, offering a clearer picture of the human toll of this broken system.

Chapter 3

Race, Bias, and Brutality

Brooks, a Black man, is one of countless inmates of color who have faced disproportionate punishment and abuse in America's correctional facilities. His case shines a light on the deeper, systemic racism that underpins much of the brutality in prisons, from glaring racial disparities in inmate treatment to biases entrenched within the correctional workforce itself.

Statistical Disparities in Punishment and Abuse

The U.S. prison system has long been criticized for its stark racial inequities. Black and Latino people make up nearly 60% of the incarcerated population, despite representing only about 30% of the general population. This overrepresentation extends to how inmates are treated behind bars, with data showing significant disparities in discipline, punishment, and abuse.

Disproportionate Disciplinary Actions

Studies have consistently found that Black and Latino inmates are more likely to be punished for minor infractions compared to white inmates. According to a 2015 analysis by The New York Times, Black and Latino inmates in New York State prisons were twice as likely to be disciplined for rule violations, often for subjective offenses such as "disrespect" or "disobedience." These disciplinary actions frequently lead to harsher outcomes, such as solitary confinement or loss of visitation rights, creating a cycle of increased isolation and vulnerability.

Higher Rates of Abuse

Reports from watchdog organizations indicate that Black and Latino inmates are also more likely to experience physical abuse at the hands of correctional officers. A 2022 investigation by the Correctional Association of New York found that inmates of color were disproportionately targeted for use-of-force incidents in state prisons. In interviews, inmates described being beaten, restrained, or otherwise mistreated for behaviors that did not warrant such extreme measures.

This pattern of abuse is not unique to New York. Across the country, Black and Latino inmates are frequently subjected to excessive force, often with little recourse for justice. The racial disparities in how punishment is meted out highlight the systemic nature of the problem—one that extends far beyond individual facilities or incidents.

Systemic Racism in the Correctional Workforce

The racial disparities in inmate treatment are deeply connected to the dynamics within the correctional workforce. In many states, the staff who oversee prisons are overwhelmingly white, while the inmate population is disproportionately Black and Latino. This racial divide creates an environment ripe for bias, power imbalances, and abuse.

Demographics of the Workforce

In New York, for example, a 2022 report revealed that 91% of correctional staff at the Marcy Correctional Facility were white, compared to a prison population that was 41% Black and 21% Latino. This disparity is not unusual; prisons in rural areas often draw their workforce from predominantly white communities, while their inmate populations come from urban areas with higher concentrations of people of color.

This demographic divide fosters a "them versus us" mentality, where inmates are seen not as individuals but as threats. Racial stereotypes and prejudices can shape how officers interact with inmates, leading to dehumanization and a greater likelihood of abuse.

The Role of Implicit Bias

Even in the absence of overt racism, implicit bias plays a significant role in perpetuating disparities. Studies have shown that individuals are more likely to perceive Black men as aggressive or threatening, even when they are not exhibiting such behavior. These biases can influence how correctional officers interpret and respond to inmate actions, resulting in harsher treatment for inmates of color.

Testimonies from Inmates and Whistleblowers

Former inmates and whistleblower officers have shared harrowing accounts of the racial dynamics within prisons. One Black inmate from a New York state facility described being singled out for frequent cell searches and disciplinary write-ups. "They were always looking for a reason to punish me," he said. "If a white guy did the same thing, it was just a warning."

A whistleblower officer, who asked to remain anonymous, recounted the pervasive use of racial slurs and demeaning language by colleagues. "It was just part of the culture," he said. "They didn't even try to hide it." This normalization of racist attitudes creates an environment where abuse becomes not only acceptable but expected.

The Intersection of Race and Violence

The racial disparities in the prison system are not just statistical anomalies—they are the product of systemic racism that permeates every level of the correctional system. From the over-policing of Black and Latino communities to the racial biases of correctional officers, these dynamics create a pipeline of injustice that culminates in incidents like the death of Robert Brooks.

When Brooks arrived at Marcy Correctional Facility, he entered a system that was already stacked against him. Reports from the facility describe a "hands-on" culture where violence was routinely used to assert control, particularly against inmates of color. The fact that no officers intervened during Brooks' beating—and that some appeared to take pleasure in it—reflects the dehumanization of Black and Latino inmates within the system.

Addressing Racial Disparities in Corrections

Confronting the racial inequities in the prison system requires both structural reforms and cultural change. Some steps that can help address these disparities include:

- **Diversifying the Workforce**: Hiring correctional staff who reflect the demographics of the inmate population can help reduce racial biases and foster better understanding.

- **Implicit Bias Training**: Providing officers with training to recognize and mitigate their biases can improve interactions with inmates.
- **Increased Oversight**: Independent oversight bodies can ensure that allegations of racial bias and abuse are investigated thoroughly.
- **Data Transparency**: Regularly publishing data on disciplinary actions, use-of-force incidents, and other metrics can help identify and address patterns of racial disparity.

These changes, while important, are only part of the solution. Addressing systemic racism within the correctional system requires a broader reckoning with the role of race in American society. The disparities in punishment and abuse faced by Black and Latino inmates are a reflection of deeper societal inequities—ones that demand urgent attention and action.

A Call to Action

This unfortunate case underscores the deadly consequences of ignoring racial disparities in the correctional system. His story is not unique, but it is a powerful reminder of the urgent need for reform. As we move forward, we must confront the uncomfortable truths about race, bias, and brutality in our prisons and work to build a system that values justice over prejudice. Only then can we ensure that the lives of inmates like Robert Brooks are treated with the dignity they deserve.

Chapter 4

The Aftermath of Abuse

When Robert Brooks was carried lifelessly from the Marcy Correctional Facility, his death was not just the end of a violent incident—it was the beginning of a cascade of pain and trauma. The toll of abuse in correctional facilities goes far beyond the moment it occurs. It lingers in the physical and psychological wounds of survivors, in the grief of families who lose loved ones, and in the ripples that extend into communities. For every victim of prison violence, there is a network of people whose lives are forever changed.

This chapter explores the aftermath of such abuse, offering a deeper understanding of its devastating consequences.

The Psychological and Physical Toll on Inmates

Physical Injuries with Lasting Impacts

The immediate physical effects of abuse are often gruesome: broken bones, internal injuries, and, in the case of Robert Brooks, fatal trauma. However, for inmates who survive such violence, the injuries often leave lasting scars—both seen and unseen.

Many survivors face chronic pain, limited mobility, or permanent disabilities due to untreated or improperly treated injuries. Inadequate medical care in prisons compounds the problem. Even when abuse is documented, many inmates are denied access to appropriate treatment, leaving them to suffer in silence.

For example, Kevin, a former inmate, described how a beating left him with a fractured rib that went untreated for months. "Every breath hurt," he said. "But when I asked for help, they just told me to tough it out." This lack of care reflects a system that often disregards the humanity of those in its custody.

Psychological Trauma and PTSD

The psychological toll of prison abuse can be equally devastating. Survivors frequently suffer from post-traumatic stress disorder (PTSD), anxiety, depression, and feelings of helplessness. The environment of constant surveillance and powerlessness only exacerbates these conditions.

One former inmate, Maria, described how the fear of further abuse haunted her long after her release. "I couldn't sleep without nightmares," she said. "Every time I saw a uniform, my heart would race. I still don't feel safe, even though I'm out."

For many inmates, the trauma is compounded by the lack of support systems within prison walls. Mental health resources are scarce, and seeking help is often stigmatized. As a result, survivors are left to navigate their pain alone, with few avenues for healing.

How Families and Communities Are Affected

The impact of abuse in prisons extends far beyond the individual victims. Families and communities also bear the weight of the violence inflicted within correctional facilities.

Families Grappling with Loss

For families like Robert Brooks', the aftermath of abuse is defined by grief and unanswered questions. The loss of a loved one in such brutal circumstances leaves a void that can never be filled.

Elizabeth Mazur, an attorney representing the Brooks family, described their anguish after watching the footage of his death. "They saw his last moments, and it was devastating," she said. "It's not just the loss—they're left wondering how this could happen, why no one stopped it, and whether justice will ever be served."

Beyond the emotional toll, families often face financial hardships as well. Legal battles, funeral costs, and the loss of a primary breadwinner can plunge families into economic uncertainty, compounding their pain.

Communities Feeling the Ripple Effect

The effects of prison abuse are felt deeply in the communities that inmates leave behind. For many neighborhoods—particularly those with high incarceration rates—the cycle of violence in prisons reinforces systemic inequalities.

Communities of color are disproportionately impacted, as they are overrepresented in the prison system. When abuse leads to death or long-term trauma, it robs these communities of fathers, mothers, siblings, and friends. The collective grief and loss further erode trust in institutions meant to uphold justice.

Stories of Survivors and Those Who Didn't Make It

The Survivors Who Speak Out

Some survivors of prison abuse find the strength to share their stories, hoping to spark change. Their testimonies are both heartbreaking and inspiring, offering a glimpse into the resilience of the human spirit.

Take Darnell, who survived a near-fatal beating in a Florida prison. Left with permanent nerve damage, he now advocates for prison reform. "What happened to me shouldn't happen to anyone," he said. "But the only way to change things is to speak up, no matter how hard it is."

For others, the scars—both physical and emotional—make speaking out impossible. Many live in silence, carrying their pain with them long after their sentences are served.

The Ones We've Lost

For every survivor, there are those who didn't make it. Stories like Robert Brooks' are tragically common, yet many go unnoticed. Families fight to keep their loved ones' memories alive, often facing an uphill battle against systems designed to obscure the truth.

One such story is that of Kalief Browder, a young man who took his own life after enduring years of abuse and solitary confinement at Rikers Island. His case became a rallying cry for reform, but it also underscored the long-term consequences of a system that inflicts trauma without accountability.

Robert Brooks' death joins this grim legacy—a stark reminder of the human cost of prison violence. His story, and those like it, demand that we confront the failures of our correctional system and the lives it continues to destroy.

The Unseen Toll

The aftermath of abuse in correctional facilities is multifaceted, affecting survivors, families, and communities in profound ways. The physical injuries may heal, but the psychological wounds often last a lifetime. The families left behind carry the weight of their loss, while communities grapple with the broader implications of systemic violence.

As this book continues, we will explore how these stories fuel the fight for change. By amplifying the voices of survivors and honoring the memories of those we've lost, we can begin to address the deeper issues within our prisons and demand a system that values humanity over brutality. The question remains: How much longer can we allow these cycles of violence to continue before we act?

Chapter 5

Calls for Reform

Robert's tragic story is not an anomaly but a reflection of systemic failures that plague the U.S. correctional system. While the challenges are immense, they are not insurmountable. Across the country and the globe, reform initiatives have shown that change is possible when there is the will to act. From body cameras and diversity training to bold policy overhauls, these efforts provide a roadmap for creating a prison system that prioritizes humanity, accountability, and justice.

Promising Initiatives for Reform

1. Body Cameras: Enhancing Transparency and Accountability

Body cameras have emerged as a key tool in increasing oversight within correctional facilities. When used properly, they provide an unbiased record of interactions between officers and inmates, deterring misconduct and aiding investigations.

In jurisdictions where body camera policies are strictly enforced, incidents of abuse have decreased significantly. For example, a pilot program in a California state prison found that body cameras reduced use-of-force incidents by 54% in just one year. However, the effectiveness of this technology depends on proper implementation. Cameras must be activated automatically, tamper-proof, and subject to regular audits to ensure compliance.

2. Diversity Training: Tackling Implicit Bias

Implicit bias among correctional staff contributes to the disproportionate abuse faced by Black and Latino inmates. Diversity training programs aim to address these biases by educating officers about cultural competence, empathy, and the impact of systemic racism.

While such training alone cannot eradicate bias, it can lay the groundwork for cultural change within correctional institutions. Programs like those implemented in Washington State's Department of Corrections have shown promise, with participating staff reporting improved relationships with inmates and a reduction in racially motivated complaints.

3. Reducing Solitary Confinement: A More Humane Approach

Solitary confinement, often used as a punitive measure, has been widely condemned for its devastating psychological effects. Reform efforts in states like New Jersey and Colorado have focused on limiting its use, particularly for vulnerable populations such as juveniles and individuals with mental illnesses.

Colorado, in particular, has been a leader in this area. Under the guidance of former corrections director Rick Raemisch, the state reduced its reliance on solitary confinement, capping its use at 15 days and emphasizing rehabilitation over punishment. The results were striking: fewer incidents of self-harm, improved inmate behavior, and a safer environment for both inmates and staff.

Success Stories from Reform Efforts

Norway: A Model of Rehabilitation

Norway's correctional system is often cited as a model for humane and effective reform. Unlike the punitive focus of U.S. prisons, Norway emphasizes rehabilitation and reintegration. Facilities like Halden Prison provide inmates with private rooms, education, job training, and access to mental health services.

The results speak for themselves: Norway boasts one of the lowest recidivism rates in the world, with only 20% of released inmates reoffending within two years. This success demonstrates that treating inmates with dignity and respect can lead to better outcomes for individuals and society as a whole.

Germany: Prison as a Community Responsibility

In Germany, prisons operate under the philosophy that deprivation of liberty is punishment enough. Inmates are given opportunities to work, study, and maintain family connections, reducing the stigma and isolation often associated with incarceration.

One standout example is Neustrelitz Prison, which offers inmates vocational training programs in fields like carpentry and automotive repair. These programs equip inmates with the skills needed to secure stable employment upon release, breaking the cycle of reoffending.

California: Addressing Use-of-Force Issues

Closer to home, California has made strides in reducing violence within its correctional facilities.

By implementing body cameras, increasing oversight, and expanding mental health services, the state has seen measurable improvements. For instance, in prisons with active reform programs, use-of-force incidents dropped by nearly half over five years.

Recommendations for Systemic Change

The path to meaningful reform requires bold and comprehensive action. Based on the successes and lessons from existing initiatives, here are key recommendations for transforming the U.S. correctional system:

1. **Mandate Body Cameras Nationwide**
   - Require all correctional officers to wear body cameras with automatic activation.

- Establish strict penalties for tampering or failure to comply with body camera policies.
    - Implement regular audits and publicly release footage in cases of alleged misconduct.
2. **Limit the Use of Solitary Confinement**
    - Cap solitary confinement to no more than 15 consecutive days, in line with international human rights standards.
    - Provide mental health services to inmates in isolation and prioritize alternative disciplinary measures.
3. **Invest in Diversity Training and Workforce Reform**
    - Implement mandatory implicit bias and cultural competence training for all correctional staff.
    - Diversify the correctional workforce to better reflect the demographics of the inmate population.
4. **Expand Rehabilitation Programs**

- Increase funding for education, job training, and mental health services within prisons.
- Focus on preparing inmates for reintegration into society, reducing recidivism rates.

5. **Strengthen Independent Oversight**
   - Establish independent bodies to investigate allegations of abuse and misconduct.
   - Ensure these agencies have the authority to impose penalties and recommend policy changes.

6. **Promote Transparency and Public Accountability**
   - Publish regular reports on use-of-force incidents, racial disparities, and disciplinary actions.
   - Involve community stakeholders in shaping correctional policies and practices.

A Vision for Change

Reforming the U.S. correctional system is no small task, but the consequences of inaction are too great to ignore. The tragic death of Robert Brooks is a reminder of the urgent need for accountability, transparency, and humanity in our prisons. By embracing bold reforms and learning from successful models, we can begin to dismantle the culture of violence and create a system that truly serves justice.

The road ahead is challenging, but it is not impossible. Change begins with recognizing the humanity of those behind bars and committing to a future where dignity and rehabilitation replace brutality and neglect.

Conclusion

A Path Forward

The death of Robert Brooks is not just a tragedy for his family; it is a stain on the very concept of justice. Prisons, intended to be places of rehabilitation and accountability, often devolve into arenas of unchecked violence and systemic abuse. When these institutions fail to uphold justice, society as a whole suffers. Trust in the legal system erodes, racial and economic disparities deepen, and the cycle of harm extends far beyond prison walls.

Yet, even in the face of such darkness, there is hope. History has shown that public outcry and collective advocacy can be powerful forces for change. The question is whether we, as a society, are willing to act.

What Society Loses When Prisons Fail to Uphold Justice

A Loss of Humanity

At the heart of every failed prison system is a disregard for the humanity of those it incarcerates. When abuse becomes normalized, the individuals behind bars are seen not as people deserving of dignity and fairness but as objects to be controlled. This dehumanization ripples outward, diminishing our collective sense of compassion and empathy.

The cost is not just moral—it is practical. Research has consistently shown that when inmates are treated with respect and provided with opportunities for rehabilitation, recidivism rates plummet. Conversely, systems rooted in violence and neglect produce individuals who are more likely to reoffend, perpetuating cycles of crime and incarceration.

Erosion of Trust in Justice

The integrity of the justice system hinges on the principle of fairness. When prisons fail to uphold this ideal, public confidence in the system collapses. Communities—particularly those disproportionately impacted by incarceration—lose faith that the law serves their interests. This mistrust extends to law enforcement, courts, and policymakers, creating deep divides between citizens and the institutions meant to protect them.

Intergenerational Harm

The impact of prison abuse does not end with the individual victim. Families and communities bear the burden of lost loved ones, economic hardship, and emotional trauma. Children of incarcerated parents often experience instability, stigma, and a higher likelihood of entering the criminal justice system themselves. This intergenerational harm exacerbates inequality and entrenches systemic injustices.

The Role of Public Outcry and Advocacy in Driving Change

Throughout history, public outcry has been a catalyst for reform. The civil rights movement, the fight for women's suffrage, and recent calls for police accountability all underscore the power of collective action. The same energy is needed to confront the failures of the prison system.

Shining a Light on Injustice

The release of body camera footage in Robert Brooks' case sparked widespread outrage, forcing officials to take action. Transparency—whether through investigative journalism, watchdog reports, or publicized video evidence—is a crucial first step in exposing systemic failures. When the public is confronted with the stark reality of abuse, complacency becomes impossible.

Advocacy and Grassroots Movements

Advocacy groups and grassroots movements play a vital role in pushing for reform. Organizations like the Correctional Association of New York, The Marshall Project, and others work tirelessly to document abuses, lobby for policy changes, and amplify the voices of those impacted by incarceration. Their efforts remind us that systemic change begins with collective pressure.

Legislative and Policy Change

Public pressure can also drive legislative reform. When constituents demand accountability, policymakers are forced to respond. Recent successes, such as the First Step Act, which aims to reduce recidivism and improve prison conditions, demonstrate the potential for meaningful progress when advocacy intersects with political will.

A Call to Action

The story of Robert Brooks should not end with outrage—it should mark the beginning of change. His death, like so many others, is a call to confront the systemic failures of our correctional system and to demand better.

We must challenge the culture of violence and dehumanization that permeates our prisons. We must advocate for transparency, accountability, and reform. And we must remember that justice is not just about punishment—it is about dignity, fairness, and the opportunity for redemption.

The path forward is clear but requires collective effort. It begins with acknowledging the humanity of those behind bars, holding institutions accountable, and refusing to accept a system that perpetuates harm. As a society, we have the power to shape a more just and compassionate future. The time to act is now.

www.ingramcontent.com/pod-product-compliance
Lightning Source LLC
Chambersburg PA
CBHW051705250726

48653CB00007B/2854